LONDON

PUBCATS

words **Vicky Lane**
photos **Tim White**

PARADISE ROAD

Cats, pubs – and a café

Lily at the Anglesea Arms, Ravenscourt Park 12

Legz at the Charlotte Despard, Archway 24

Duchess at the Duke of Hamilton, Hampstead 34

Molly & Smoky at the Eight Bells, Putney 42

Purdy at the Gunmakers, Marylebone 52

Donnie & friends at Lady Dinah's Cat Emporium, Shoreditch 62

Billie & Herman at the Nags Head, Walthamstow 72

Winnie & Churchill at the Old Eagle, Camden 82

Salem at the Pelton Arms, Greenwich 92

Lenny & Patch at the Pride of Spitalfields, Brick Lane 100

Betty & Beyoncé at the Rose & Crown, Clapham 108

Pork Pie & Scratchings at the Southampton Arms, Gospel Oak 116

Nelson at the Tapping the Admiral, Kentish Town 126

Horacio & Woody at the Trinity Arms, Brixton 138

Craig at the Westow House, Crystal Palace 148

Bud at the White Bear, Farringdon 156

Biscuit & Tea at the White Swan & Cuckoo, Wapping 162

More cats and pubs 172

London, pubs and cats

THIS IS A BOOK ABOUT CATS that live in pubs in London. Why? Because we like cats, we like pubs and we live in London, where our flats are often too small for cats of our own. We put up with these mean living spaces in the hope that somewhere down the line we will earn enough to be able to afford a proper place, a house, maybe with a garden. But try explaining that to a cat. Cats are not interested in long-term goals. So we do not have a cat because keeping it cooped up in a tiny flat seems cruel.

Lauren Pears, an Australian living in London, came up with a smart idea. In 2014, she opened the city's first cat café, where people who didn't have cats of their own could come and spend some time with the café's cats. Which is terrific,

except there is only so much tea and coffee a person can consume. Unlike beer, which can be consumed in limitless quantities. How much better if you could drink beer and play with a cat at the same time. Well, of course, you can.

London loves cats. The city is full of tales of notable felines stretching back to medieval mayor Richard Whittington and his nameless (and possibly fictional) cat. The connection between cats and high office continues today with an official Chief Mouser to the Cabinet Office in residence at 10 Downing Street (the present incumbent is Larry). This is a continuation of a tradition that dates back to the time of Henry VIII.

Away from the skirting boards of power, a revered cat called Hodge belonging to distinguished man-of-letters Samuel Johnson is commemorated by a very fine bronze statue just off Fleet Street. More recently, a bronze was unveiled of Sam the Cat in Queen Square Gardens in Holborn, honouring the pet of a former local resident and campaigner. More than one West End theatre has a tradition of keeping working cats, as have several of the mainline railway stations. Barbican Underground station used to have Pebbles, a cat that sat all day on the ticket barriers, alert to fare dodgers. The British Museum used to have Mike, a cat that patrolled its galleries, while St Paul's Church in Covent Garden currently has two cats, Inigo and Jones, although neither is ordained. No surprise then that numerous London pubs would have cats, too.

We already knew about Tom Paine at Holborn's Seven Stars – sadly dearly departed before this book got underway – and the cats at Whitechapel's Blind Beggar. Once we started asking around we learned of lots more. A workmate told us about the Boogaloo, home to Starsky and Hutch, and another pointed us to the kittens at the Old Eagle in Camden. A chance conversation alerted us to a three-legged cat in Archway, and someone else remembered a pub in Walthamstow that had hosted a wedding for two of its cats. (Another friend remembered that way back, long before the alcohol ban on London Underground, when there even used to be pubs at some of the stations, the pub on the westbound platform at Sloane Square – now a snack shop – also had a pubcat.)

Making the acquaintance of the pubcats was a delight. Publicans and bar staff tend to be talkative sorts anyway, it's the nature of the job, and once you get them started on their cats… We're "one little family," said Ash Millard, manager of the Southampton Arms in Gospel Oak, where the family includes two silvery-blue British shorthairs. The familial vibe often extends to the pub regulars, who can be touchingly protective of the smallest member of the clan. "That's Salem's spot – sit there and you'll have us lot on your case," a drinker at the Pelton Arms warned us, Salem being the pub's cranky old puss.

What is heartening is how for many of the cats the pub has been a sort of salvation. Several of the cats in this book were rescue cats given a home by a benevolent pub owner; others were strays that took it on themselves to adopt a pub and have been at home there ever since. These cats have gone from what was possibly a forlorn existence to becoming mascots of their new abodes and the centre of constant attention. It is not a bad gig: space to roam and come and go as you like, regular meals plus tidbits from customers' plates, and the pick of the venue's seating. The downside is having to endure endless strokes and ear scratches from customers when all you want to do is nap, but there are worse ways to live. 🐾

Duke of Hamilton
🚇 HAMPSTEAD

Southampton Arms
🚆 GOSPEL OAK

Hampstead

Kentish Town

Tapping the Admiral
🚇 KENTISH TOWN

Old Eagle
🚆 CAMDEN ROAD

Regents Park

Gunmakers
🚇 BAKER STREET

Shepherd's Bush

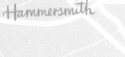

Hyde Park

BUCKINGHAM PALACE

BIG BEN

Anglesea Arms
🚇 RAVENSCOURT PARK

Hammersmith

Chelsea

BATTERSEA POWER STATION

Clapham

Fulham

Eight Bells
🚇 PUTNEY BRIDGE

Rose & Crown
🚇 CLAPHAM COMMON

Trinity Arms
🚇 BRIXTON

Putney

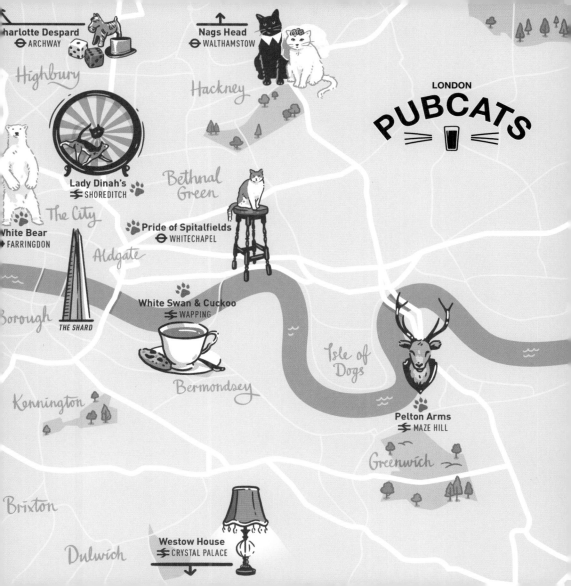

LONDON

PUBCATS

Charlotte Despard
⬤ ARCHWAY

Highbury

Nags Head
⬤ WALTHAMSTOW

Hackney

Lady Dinah's
⮂ SHOREDITCH

Bethnal
Green

The City

White Bear
⮂ FARRINGDON

Aldgate

Pride of Spitalfields
⬤ WHITECHAPEL

THE SHARD

Borough

White Swan & Cuckoo
⮂ WAPPING

Isle of
Dogs

Pelton Arms
⮂ MAZE HILL

Kennington

Bermondsey

Greenwich

Brixton

Westow House
⮂ CRYSTAL PALACE

Dulwich

Lily

The most loyal regular at Ravenscourt Park's Anglesea Arms enjoys a pint of prawns not beer

FOR A LONG TIME, Lily was a bit of a mystery cat. Although she can be found at the Anglesea Arms most days, she doesn't actually live there. But when live-in Australian deputy-manager Kathryn Wild comes down to get the pub ready for the day, somewhere around 11am Lily will usually appear outside the window, peering in, patiently waiting for someone to open the front door for her.

If Kathryn is not around, then the cleaner will usually oblige.

The elderly feline – who is predominately white with patches of rusty-brown and black on her face, and a raccoon-like, bushy striped tail – will usually spend most of each day inside, curled up on the shelf of a mirrored, wood-panelled pillar facing the door or, in colder weather, sleeping on

ANGLESEA ARMS
35 Wingate Road, W6 (Ravenscourt Park tube)
📞 020 8749 1291
🐦 AngleseaArmsW6
📘 theangleseaarmsW6
🌐 www.angleseaarmspub.co.uk

FACILITIES Exhibits and sells the work of local artists, outside seating, real fire

DRINKS Global wine list, decent selection of real ales

FOOD High-end gastro pub selling locally sourced, seasonal produce. Menu changes daily

one of the big leather sofas beside the fire. She is such a fixture that she has her own food bowl, which gets filled twice a day. It sits below and to the left of her portrait, painted by local artist Jenny Abbott. As the pub doesn't open until 5pm Monday to Thursday, she's left undisturbed all afternoon. Later on, she grudgingly shares her domain with the paying customers. She used to get a little gnarly with anyone who disturbed her, but she has mellowed with age, says Kathryn. Then each evening, come closing time, she departs. "She might be sleeping but I just have to say 'Lily, it's time,' and she'll get up and leave straight away," says manager Chris Welburn.

The mystery was, where did she go? That was solved when a customer came in and identified

Lily as her cat. She lives locally, although she spends far more time at the pub than at home. When her owner comes in, Lily always acts as though she doesn't know her.

It is a very cat-friendly neighbourhood. The Anglesea is within what estate agents call Brackenbury Village, a network of pretty terraced streets lined with affluent homes, boutiquey shops and not much traffic. The pub itself is a handsome place, particularly following a four-month refurb in 2014 when the place was taken over by new owners George and Richard Manners. Predating their arrival, the pub had a solid reputation as one of London's original gastropubs, and it still has an excellent kitchen serving lunch Friday, Saturday, Sunday, and dinner seven nights a week.

The Manners brothers own six independent pubs across south-west London, each with its own character. There is one thing they all have in common: like the Anglesea, the Cumberland Arms and Dartmouth Castle, both in Hammersmith, the Swan in Chiswick, Atlas in Fulham, and Fox & Hounds on Latchmere Road in Battersea all have cats. Not all of them are as comfortable around people as Lily and some keep to the staff quarters upstairs, never venturing into the bar.

No one knows for sure how old Lily is, though Kathryn suspects she's "getting on" because she sometimes has difficulty seeing her food. "We now have to rattle her bowl to let her know where it is," says Kathryn. Lily still, however, maintains her peculiar habit of flipping the biscuits out of her

"She has in the past leapt onto a table and attempted to swipe a customer's prawns"

bowl, one by one, before eating them. What she really loves, though, are prawns. She has in the past leapt onto a customer's table and attempted to swipe the crustaceans. She isn't allowed in the dining room, a rule that she respects, but people can order food to eat in the bar and regulars sometimes buy her a half-pint glass of prawns of her own. That can get a bit messy as Lily prefers that you peel the prawns for her.

Brisbane-native Kathryn, who started at the pub at the end of 2014, says it's partly Lily's fault she's still in the UK: "The plan had been to work the summer and then go travelling but I grew too attached to Lily," she confesses. "I've just moved in upstairs and my plan now is to entice Lily up there to join me, permanently." 🐾

Legz

The three-legged cat that lives at Archway's Charlotte Despard has a fanbase that extends far beyond the north London pub

THE CHARLOTTE DESPARD is the most excellent of pubs. Its owners Chris Sparks and Amber Knight have, in the four years since they took up the lease, overcome a grim location on the speedway that is north London's Archway Road to create a haven of conviviality. The bar provides a top-rank line-up of beers mostly from independent local producers, while the pub itself is a large den filled with music, games, books and TV – the perfect place for regulars to unwind each evening (the pub opens at 5pm weekdays) and at weekends. While it may not look it, Archway is rapidly gentrifying, a home to City and media folk, who also make up the core regulars here – radio DJ Chris Moyles drops by from time to time, as do a couple of actors from *Game of Thrones*.

The Charlotte Despard also has the most remarkable of cats. His name is Legz, which is intentionally ironic as he doesn't have the full set. He was handed in as a stray to a vet after being hit by a car, an accident which cost him one of his limbs and required him to have his jaw wired. Once on the mend, he went through a series of rehoming schemes, but no one wanted him. That is, until one of the Charlotte Despard's regulars alerted Amber and Chris to the triped's plight after seeing him on Twitter.

"We used to live upstairs with two other cats, Goose and Hendricks," says Amber. "They were the original pub cats." However, when Amber and Chris moved out of the pub and into a house in East Finchley, they took their pets, leaving a

CHARLOTTE DESPARD
17–19 Archway Road, N19 (Archway tube)
☎ 020 7272 7872
🖾 TheDespard
🆆 www.thecharlottedespard.co.uk

FACILITIES Board games, book club and library, darts, DJ nights, jukebox, newspapers, pool table, quiz night (Tue), video games, wifi

DRINKS Extensive line-up of real ales and craft beers on draught mostly from local independent producers, plus around 65 imported bottled craft ales in the fridges and a similarly well-selected wine list

FOOD Bar snacks only

vacancy in the pub. "When we heard about this poor, three-legged puss that nobody wanted we thought, why not give him a home here."

When he arrived, in February 2014, the couple thought it would be best to close the pub for his first 24 hours in residence. The second night was quiz night and the pub was packed. "He loved it," says Amber. "He was wandering around, sitting on people's tables, lapping up the attention." He has not left the pub since and sleeps on the premises.

When he's not stretched out on the glass washer or the radiator by the front window, Legz struts around or sits up at the bar, letting everybody know who's boss. Being a quarter deficient in the leg department in no way hinders his movement, or dampens his curiosity. He loves

"Some nights Chris will present Legz with three beers and the one he chooses is discounted for the night"

engaging with people. "He's a man's cat," she says. "He likes a lot of rough and tumble." He was probably wild for the first five years of his life, before the accident, reckons Chris.

Since settling at the pub, Legz has been featured in the local newspapers and in a Japanese cat book. In 2014 he was awarded the prestigious title of Rescue Cat of the Year in the National Cat Awards. People now turn up at the Charlotte Despard specially to meet him, bringing treats and toys. Chris and Amber even encourage customers to bring their own cats to meet Legz (dogs are banned from the pub).

One treat off limits, though, is pork scratchings; Legz discovered these in the pub one night after hours and ate three whole packets in one go.

"That's the equivalent of ninety-six kilos of fat," says Amber. "He was so ill. Since then it's been no more scratchings for him."

Chris involves Legz in the running of the pub wherever he can. Some nights he'll present him with three glasses of beer and the one Legz chooses is discounted for the night.

Legz is also a fan of DJ Liz Wheatley, who spins classic soul and funk on the first Saturday of the month with Legz installed next to the decks. "He's not that bothered about Stevie Wonder or stuff like that but his ears prick up for West Coast hip hop."

For Chris, those Saturdays sum up the key to keeping a happy pub: "If you can get people dancing and playing with your cat, then that's what it's about." 🐾

Duchess

**A Hampstead cat, resident at the grand
old Duke of Hamilton, with a liking for
the theatre and churchyards**

ONE OF THE OLDEST PUBS in London, dating
back to the early 1700s, the Duke of Hamilton is
a five-minute walk up from the tube station along
swanky Hampstead High Street. It's a raffishly
handsome place, with a guardsman's-red
Georgian frontage set up a short flight of steps
from the street, and stables round the back for
any cavaliers who might happen to drop by.

Since 2011, the pub has been run by Steve
Coxshall, who leads a double life as a manager of
music acts – he used to handle pop group Blue.
But behind every grand duke there's invariably a
grand duchess.

This Duke's particular lady put herself forward
for the role, strutting into the pub one day a few
months after Coxshall's arrival. Sporting a lush

DUKE OF HAMILTON
23-25 New End, NW3 (Hampstead tube)
📞 020 7794 2068
🐦 dukeofhamilton
🅦 www.thedukeofhamilton.com

FACILITIES Beer terrace, board games, darts; basement theatre with live comedy, jazz, magic, music, open-mic nights and theatre (www.rabbitholenw3.com)

DRINKS Decent selection of six real ales, befitting a regular fixture in the *Good Beer Guide*. It also claims to offer the cheapest pint in Hampstead

FOOD Traditional British food, weekend BBQ

white coat with ginger and black patches, she turned up looking worse for wear, but she padded to the bar and hopped up onto a stool, and she's been around ever since.

"There was no other name for her but Duchess," says manager Joey Cassidy. It's a good fit, he says, because she is a cat with an attitude. She will take a swipe at customers who try to pick her up and she is generally a bit sniffy with women. "They're competition," says Ben, a Duke regular who finds favour with the Duchess.

Joey, who lives above the pub, definitely finds her demanding: pre-dawn wake-ups are a regular thing as most nights he's disturbed by a relentless meowing outside his bedroom window. He has to

This is Cocky
(The Owners) Seat!

Donate £1 To
Great Ormond St.
For The Privilege
To Sit Here!

or sit here at Your own Risk

get out of bed and let Duchess in. She sometimes enters with a gift of a mouse or bird, once even a squirrel. "She likes to sleep on the top shelf of my wardrobe after a night's hunting," he explains.

Downstairs in the pub, she is well known for suddenly flipping out mid-sleep. "She'll suddenly wake up and start chasing her tail round," says Joey. Ben has a theory: "It's Oliver Reed channeling his spirit through her," he says. The hell-raising actor, of *Oliver!* and *Gladiator* fame, used to drop by the Duke of Hamilton when he was in London, sometimes bringing along friends like Peter O'Toole or Richard Burton.

Reed's is not the only famous name associated with the pub. "Ed Sheeran used to play downstairs in the Rabbit Hole a lot before he got big," says

Joey, referring to the theatre-space in the pub's basement, where music and comedy are put on several nights a week. "He's a mate of Steve's," he explains. Guitarist and singer/songwriter Ryan Keen has also played a few gigs here, while members of Blue still sometimes show their faces.

In similar fashion, although Duchess is firmly associated with the pub, there is no guarantee she will necessarily be around when you visit. She comes and goes as she pleases. She will often slip out the door to roam the neighbourhood and prowl the nearby churchyard. She will also occasionally disappear down the Rabbit Hole. "There's been a number of times I've gone to clear up and found white hairs all over the theatre seats," says Joey. "Bloody Duchess has been down there again." 🐾

Molly & Smoky

**Down by the river in Putney at the venerable
Eight Bells, a new kitten competes for attention
with the established queen of the bar**

THOMAS DIGNAM must really love his wife Sue.
The couple have been married for 40 years now
– that's four decades of good times and bad,
sickness and health, and for Thomas, who
"doesn't really care for animals", of accepting his
wife's obsession with cats. "They used to call me
the cat lady," says Sue, with a cackle, "And they
were right, I am."

Back in the Isle of Man, when the couple ran the
Railway Station Hotel in Port St Mary for 12 years,
Sue had more than 20 cats. She was the self-
appointed, unofficial carer for the island's wild
feline population. She renovated two sheds at the
back of her pub to become feeding and sleeping
stations for her herd of feral pets, all of which she
claims she knew individually and all of which she

EIGHT BELLS
89 Fulham High Street, SW6 (Putney Bridge tube)
☎ 020 7736 6307

FACILITIES Outdoor seating, takeaway coffee, TV sports

DRINKS A big selection of lagers but only two real ales on draught

FOOD Home-made pub grub including Sunday roasts

gave names. The return, she says, was "the best pub pest control in the world".

For the last 15 years, the couple have run the Eight Bells, which is tucked away round the corner from Putney Bridge tube station, across the road from a Premier Inn and facing All Saints Fulham church. The urban location mitigates against large-scale cat enterprises so, instead, Sue runs an unofficial wild-cat protection scheme when the couple visit their holiday home in Albir, on Spain's Costa Blanca, twice a year. Back in Putney she has to be content with just the two cats, one of which, a kitten called Smoky, is a recent transplant from Spain, brought back to the UK as a souvenir from Sue's 2015 summer vacation. "I knew the second I saw him that I wanted him," she admits.

"He's the most gorgeous blue colour and I was instantly smitten."

After "trying him out" in the holiday apartment and finding that he was very comfortable with the idea of being domesticated – something, she explains, you can only do to a wild cat under the age of 10 weeks – Sue started procedures to get the tiny, Spanish *gatito* back to England. Masses of paperwork, vaccinations, a kitty-passport, a two-and-a-half day drive and £800 later – and Smoky was a resident of riverside south-west London.

He has a lovely home: the Eight Bells claims to have been licensed to sell alcohol since 1629, although back then it was called the Blue Anchor and was a wholly different building. The current

pub, which dates from the 18th century, greets punters with hanging flower baskets and lattice windows. Inside, the pub is just one room small with a bar like a ship's stern and walls hung with nautical prints (the river is just a stone's throw away). Back in the 1880s the pub served as the changing room for the players of what would become Fulham FC and current ground Craven Cottage is nearby (the pub gets packed on match days). In recent times, the Eight Bells is where indie band The Vaccines wrote their first two albums and conducted their first-ever interview, lead singer Justin Hayward-Young told London's *Time Out* magazine.

While playful new arrival Smoky has been a hit with big-hearted staff and regular customers, not everyone has been quite so welcoming. Molly, the pub's long-standing – and usually amicable – pub

"They used to call me the cat lady," says Sue, with a cackle. "And they are right, I am"

cat of 14 years standing, is less keen. The chunky tabby is the long-established queen of the Eight Bells and rightly possessive of her territory: just ask pub pugs Steven Gerrard and Chelsea, who Sue says are terrified of her. Ditto mice: "She can smell a mouse from miles away. She'll stay downstairs to patrol the pub overnight and then she lines up her catches for me at the bottom of the stairs."

Still, Molly better get used to company because Sue hopes to eventually breed the beautiful blue kitten, which, of course, means at some point finding a suitable female for Smoky. "Yes, I'll have to get another one," she says. "Just don't tell Thomas." 🐾

Purdy

Marylebone's Gunmakers has undergone changes of management and name, but one constant has been the pub's picky cat

IT IS A SHAME Purdy the cat can't talk. If he could, the long, slender black puss would surely have a whole, well, catalogue of anecdotes from his years at the Gunmakers. He may even be able to shed some light on how this pub, a block back from boutique-lined Marylebone High Street, became his home. Because currently he is the only one who knows for sure.

"We think he's eight or nine years old though that's just a guess," says current manager Annette Uiga. "The problem is that many managers and even owners have come and gone, while Purdy has stayed put."

What everybody does know, though, is that whoever introduced the cat to the pub – a modestly sized, woody, L-shaped room that fills

with an after-work crowd, weekend sports fans and visitors to the farmers' market held each Sunday in the car park in front – taught him high standards. The fussy animal will only eat the most expensive brands of cat food and stages hunger strikes if lesser offerings are placed in his bowl.

He is never interested in the food served to customers but he does enjoy the treats that the staff keep for him – although these had to be halted last year when Purdy developed a waddle. "He got a bit fat and we had to put him on a diet," says Annette. "He really didn't like that."

He's back to normal size now, which allows him to indulge in one of his favourite games, which is hiding in tight places to surprise people. "You'll go

GUNMAKERS
33 Aybrook Street, W1 (Baker Street tube)
☎ 020 7487 4987
🔲 gunmakersw1
🅵 GunmakersMarylebone

FACILITIES BT/Sky Sports, outdoor seating, quiz (Mon), upstairs function room

DRINKS Four real ales on draught plus craft beers

FOOD Classic British pub grub

down into the cellar to grab some crisps and suddenly a paw will burst out of the hole in the box and take a swipe at you." He also likes hiding on the top shelf in the pub's office, waiting to pounce on anyone who reaches up.

His other notable habit is starting each working day with a drink. Whichever member of staff is setting up before opening has to fill a pint glass with water and place it at the end of the bar. "He loves drinking out of a glass," says Annette. "He's good company, too, we all chat to him while we work, just like any regular."

Purdy will then curl up on one of the pub's red-leather-upholstered benches and get a quick 40 winks before the first customers arrive to disturb him. Past cat-botherers have included

"He's good company," *says Annette. "We all talk to him while we work"*

Eddie Redmayne and Kirsten Dunst, who have dropped in the pub following a visit to the Working Title Films' offices next door.

The most prominent famous face at the pub though is that of Winston Churchill, with three portraits of him adorning the walls. One pair flanks framed decorative displays of vintage cartridges and bullets, a nod to the pub's name, chosen by the current owner, Jim McCarthy, a man with an interest in British history – prior to Jim's arrival, this was the Scottish-themed William Wallace.

Purdy has a notably unwarlike temperament. Annette says she once watched a mouse run into him and scamper away again unbothered by any paw swipe – in fact, the cat barely blinked. Mice are not gourmet, obviously. 🐾

Donnie & friends

Okay, it is not a pub but Lady Dinah's Cat Emporium in Shoreditch is the place to go if you love the company of cats

IT IS DIFFICULT TO TALK to Lauren Pears. It is not that the bubbly Australian owner of Lady Dinah's – the UK's first cat café – is standoffish or anything, it's just that minutes after we meet she becomes a human cat-table. She bends at the stomach so Donnie, a white-and-ginger American shorthair, can perform his party trick of standing on her back. Lauren and Donnie are immediately surrounded by the 15 or so visitors to the cat café, who get up from their own boringly inanimate white wrought-iron tables to snap photographs on their mobile phones.

"I find it hard to concentrate when there's a cat around," Lauren says from an awkward, 90-degree angle. "They distract me too much." Which must pose a considerable problem considering she

LADY DINAH'S CAT EMPORIUM
152-154 Bethnal Green Road, E2 (Liverpool Street
Station tube or Shoreditch High Street Overground)
📞 020 7729 0953
🐦 LadyDinahsCats
📘 LadyDinahsCatEmporium
🌐 www.ladydinahs.com

FACILITIES Cat yoga classes, colouring-in with cats,
pet first-aid courses, gift shop

RULES The cats are in charge here: no picking up,
no feeding, no pestering and no flash photography.
Let them come to you

FOOD & DRINK Coffee, tea and cake, plus breakfast,
soups, salads, stews and bagels

shares her two-level tearoom with up to 12 of
them. They loll on the "grassy" shelves that are
fixed to the walls; poke both ends out of dainty
cat-houses; repose on cat-beds (or, more
accurately, cat chaise longues); exercise in the
giant cat-wheel; or stretch across the middle of
the wooden floor.

The result of a hugely successfully (and highly
publicised) crowd-funding campaign that racked
up almost £110,000 in three months, Lady Dinah's
owes its genesis to a bad day at work. Lauren was
a senior project manager working in computer
games who, after a miserable day at the office,
had her mood lightened on the way home by the
affections of a stray cat. "It made me realise that

everything seems better when there's a cat," the 33-year-old explains. "I wrote my business plan the next day."

The dream was to create a place where people who didn't have a cat of their own would be able to come and enjoy the tonic of feline company. A tough year of campaigning, property searching, licensing difficulties and visa problems had to be endured before Lady Dinah's finally opened its east London doors in March 2014. (It's named after Alice's kitten in Lewis Carroll's *Alice in Wonderland*.)

Within its first year of opening, Lady Dinah's had more than 65,000 visitors, 20,000 of whom booked in the first week. "We were getting

booking requests for a year ahead which was ridiculous. It also meant anyone just showing up had no chance of getting in," says Lauren. Walk-in slots have now been introduced.

The Emporium's first residents were Mue and her kittens Artemis, Biscuit, Carbonelle, Donnie, Indiana, Petra and Romeo. Mue and her litter were adopted from a family who were leaving the country and who had tried to take the cats to a shelter, but had been turned away because it was full. It all happened a little faster than Lauren would have liked: at the time the café was still a building site so the cats had to be temporarily accommodated in her flat. Once the café was up and running, Wookie and his mother, Lucy, were

CATTE............£2·50
CAT WHITE......£2·50
CATTUCCINO...£2·50
AMEOWRICANO..£2·20
MOCAT............£2·60
ESPURRESSO £2·00

taken in after their owner passed away, and Lizzie and Alice were adopted from a private shelter as replacements for cats that Lauren has allowed to be rehomed with customers with whom they'd developed a close bond.

Managing customer expectations is her biggest problem, she says. "It can be frustrating when you get comments like, 'The cats didn't do anything, they were just sleeping.' I have to remind people that they're just cats and this is their home. They're not here to perform."

They often do, though, because being cats they crave attention. On the day I visit it's not very long before half-Persian, half-tabby and wholly fluffy Wookie struts across the floor in a showy catwalk. Simultaneously, Petra, a

white-and-brown natural show-off performs leaps between shelves and little black-with-white-socks cutie Lizzie rattles around in the big wheel, meowing excitedly as she runs. It's just one big cat cabaret.

Then, of course, there's Donnie and his back-surfing antics. Like a parent, a carer for multiple cats probably should not have favourites but Lauren can't help it. "Donnie has always been really attached to my fiancé and me," she says. "Once a cat chooses you, it's such a nice thing, it ends up going both ways very quickly and he's now my favourite little buddy, too."

The contentedly purring cat still perched upon her back has obviously got his claws into her. Literally. 🐾

Billie & Herman

**As well as two pubcats, Walthamstow's
Nags Head has cat murals, cat
funerals and cat weddings**

IF YOU EVER FIND YOURSELF in Walthamstow
Village, mention the Nags Head to any local and
chances are you'll be asked, "You mean the cat
pub?" It's a response that makes Flossie Parsons
very happy.

Flossie swapped a market stall in Camden Lock,
where she sold her own hand-decorated T-shirts,
for a far more ambitious project: the makeover of a
rundown pub at the endmost stop on the
Underground's Victoria line.

Walthamstow Village is a small slice of genteel
old England, all greengrocers and sponge cakes,
dropped into gritty north-east London. It has lovely
shops and cafés, a 12th-century church, a
15th-century half-timbered Ancient House and
the excellent Vestry House and William Morris

"There were bridesmaids in dresses, a tiered wedding cake, and a miniature veil and bow tie for the happy cat couple"

museums. Set among all of this, the Nags Head has almost the air of a country pub: it is a large, cream building of rustic appearance, fronted by an appealing drinking area with bench tables and potted plants. It's only close up that you start to notice the less traditional elements, such as the silhouettes of buxom females laughing suggestively from the corners of the upstairs windows (this is the Madam La Zonga lounge) and the cat fresco. The latter is halfway up the front wall of the pub and is a line-up of four portraits, representing the pub's cats, past and present.

The first was Blackie, the cat that Flossie and her ex-partner adopted when they first took on the pub 13 years ago. He was, says Flossie, a "real gangster", throwing his weight around, scratching the ankles of kitchen staff and commanding the bar. He became a regular at the pub's social events, including their wine-tasting evenings. "He liked a nice Merlot," says Flossie. Customers adored him and when he died at the ripe old age of 18 in 2007, there was a real sense of loss. Which is why the landlady decided to give the old boy a proper send-off.

She organised a cat funeral with a New Orleans-style parade of mourners dressed in black, some hymn singing, and a few spoken tributes celebrating the life of the cherished four-legged ex-pub fixture. Unsurprisingly, the event caught the attention of first the local press and then was picked up nationally and subsequently reported across the country. "It was

NAGS HEAD
9 Orford Road, E17 (Walthamstow tube)
📞 020 8520 9709
🐦 Thenagshead_E17
📘 The-Nags-Head-Pub-Walthamstow-village
🌐 www.thenagshead17.com

FACILITIES Beer garden, community classes (pilates, wine tasting, life drawing), DJ nights (every other Fri), live jazz (Sun pm), quiz (Mon), upstairs function room

DRINKS Eight real ales on draught, good selection of bottled ciders, hand-picked wine list

FOOD Largely Italian menu with roasts on Sundays

nice to see Blackie getting the attention he deserved," says Flossie.

A neighbour's cat, called Tetley, who often popped into the Nags Head, was given similar honours when he passed. Blackie, meanwhile, was replaced at the pub by Billie, a tabby kitten who turned up three months after the first funeral – Flossie believes she was sent by Blackie. She was an immediate hit, not least with Harvey, a stunning, long-haired grey Norwegian Forest cat from next door. "They have a genuine love for each other," says Flossie.

With a certain inevitability, two cat funerals were followed by a cat wedding. Flossie pulled out all the stops. There were bridesmaids in specially made dresses, a tiered wedding cake, and a

miniature veil and bow tie for the happy couple. Flossie reckons she spent thousands on the event – even if it all got a bit much for groom Harvey, who legged it out the bathroom window within the first hour (the couple have worked through the incident, we've been assured). It was worth the money and effort, says Flossie, as the pub was the busiest it has ever been, with punters spilling out into the road. It made local headlines again, even if it was slightly overshadowed by another wedding that took place the same day – that of Prince William and Kate Middleton.

It's a shame the Nags Head's other current feline resident, tabby Herman, missed his pub-mate's big day. He turned up soon after, in the summer of 2012 and decided to stick around, probably because staff, thinking he was Billie (the two are nearly identical in appearance) were feeding him. "Everyone just assumed Billie had got greedy in matrimony," laughs Flossie.

Billie and Herman now share the pub. It' is a bright and airy place, which, with its cream-painted rustic woodwork and schoolroom furniture feels a bit like a village hall. Except how many

village halls are hung with a mix of pictures that takes in camp icons, toy dolls and, of course, cats? (And how many village halls have a ban on children? A ban strictly enforced at the Nags Head.) Herman favours the couches under the main windows (this is where he sleeps at night) and, in clement weather, the benches on the forecourt; Billie has no particular attachments and sleeps upstairs.

Quite where Harvey fits in these days in this odd ménage à trois is unclear. How does one go about staging a cat divorce? 🐾

Winnie & Churchill

It's overloaded with both character and characters, but at Camden's Old Eagle it's the two kittens that are the centre of attention

DON'T LET ANYONE tell you different: gruff Jimmy McGrath is a softy at heart. The big Irishman with unruly eyebrows is a well-known personality around north London. He's lived locally for the majority of his 75 years and in that time has owned and run many of the area's most popular boozers. Unsurprisingly, he has a fund of stories and could bend your ear for hours. Except these

days he finds himself vying for attention on his own premises, which is music pub the Old Eagle. It has been the case ever since one of his regulars came in during the first days of 2015 with a belated Christmas present: a box containing two tiny, black-and-white kittens. Newborn siblings, they had been rejected by their mother and the man wanted to know if the landlord would take

OLD EAGLE
251 Royal College St, NW1 (Camden Road Overground)
📞 020 7482 6021
🐦 oldeaglecamden
📘 oldeaglecamden

FACILITIES Beer garden, live music (Wed & Fri), table tennis

DRINKS Three real ales and you'd imagine a decent Guinness

FOOD Full Thai menu

them. "Well, I couldn't just ignore two little orphan babbies, could I?" says McGrath.

From then on, the first thing many of the pub's customers would ask when they came in was, "Where are the kittens?" "Some days there is literally a queue of people for the cats," says McGrath. "Everyone bloody loves them."

They were given the names Winston and Churchill, until someone noticed one of them was missing a certain something, requiring a name change to Winnie. You can easily tell them apart because Winnie has the black chin.

Their home is a characterful place. Round the corner from Camden Road Overground station, it is far enough from the over-touristed crush of the

"Some days there is literally a queue for the cats," says landlord Jimmy McGrath

High Street to remain a proper locals' haunt, with a cast of regulars deserving of their own reality TV show. The pub is the perfect set, its windows strung with a miscellany of battle-scarred musical instruments, wooden shoe moulds dangling from the ceiling and the walls hung with an odd collection of paintings bought by McGrath at the local auctions he enjoys frequenting. It is best experienced on Whiskey Wednesdays, the name given to the weekly sessions when a makeshift and changeable line-up of quality players gathers for an evening of giddy Irish folk music.

The cats like the red-and-blue-damask-cushioned bench opposite the bar, which is where they generally receive their adoring public – when they're not scampering around, trotting up and

down the bar, crawling up customers' legs or squeezing between pints on tables. In decent weather, they head outside to the beer garden to chase stray ping-pong balls (there is a table-tennis table out here) or just curl up in a plant pot.

It is a shame the kittens never got to meet the pub's most famous former customer, Amy Winehouse. She used to live just up the road and, according to McGrath, came in the Old Eagle a lot. He says she was "great fun" but really poor at table tennis. "I'd tell her she was useless and she'd tell me to shut it," says McGrath. Still, if Winehouse was around, that would mean even less attention for McGrath, right? No, he says: "She would have been all over those cats. They'd have kept her quiet." 🐾

Salem

At the heart of East Greenwich is the welcoming Pelton Arms and at the heart of the Pelton Arms is a not-always-so-welcoming big black cat

SALEM THE CAT does not tolerate fools. The big, black Bombay is old enough (16 and showing it) to know what he likes. "He's funny about boring people," says manager Jason Macey. "If someone's dull, he'll turn his back on them."

But he must love life at the Pelton Arms because he chose it. He just turned up one day four years ago in the garden of the East Greenwich pub. "The girls working here pleaded to keep him, then a few regulars took a liking, too," says Jason. "That's how it started."

The Pelton is a large pub 15 minutes' walk the other side of the Old Royal Naval College from central Greenwich. It sits near the river at the heart of a network of residential streets much beloved of filmmakers looking for an old-London feel. Parts of

On Saturday nights during the football season Salem watches Match of the Day *with Jason over a shared plate of pastrami*

PELTON ARMS
23-25 Pelton Road, SE10 (Maze Hill rail)
📞 020 8858 0572
🐦 peltonarms
📘 The-Pelton-Arms-Pub
🔲 www.peltonarms.com

FACILITIES Bar billiards, beer garden, knitting club (Wed), live music (Thur–Sun), quiz nights (Tue & occasional Thur)

DRINKS Fine selection of up to 10 real ales on draught, continental lagers

FOOD Classic British menu including Sunday roasts

the 1990 film *The Krays* were shot around here and so was the TV show *Rock & Chips*, about the early days of Rodney Trotter from *Only Fools and Horses*. The Pelton actually appeared in that, renamed the Nags Head for the filming, and the owners have left the fake signage in place on one facade.

The pub is very much at the heart of the local community (it hosts a knitting group!) and is known for its live music – Glenn Tilbrook of Squeeze has played here loads of times.

The pub used to have two cats called Trigger and Denzil, named for characters from *Only Fools and Horses*, but they departed when pub-owner Geoff Keen moved out. Salem was a warmly welcomed replacement.

First, Jason had to make sure the new staffer didn't belong somewhere else, so he posted "Found cat" flyers around the area. It turned out someone was missing a large black cat but when his owner turned up and saw how happy he was, she decided to leave him be.

Oddly, Salem – named after the black cat in *Sabrina the Teenage Witch* – never wanted to come inside; instead, he made his home on a sofa in the pub's outdoor smoking area. "However much we tried, he wouldn't step foot in the pub," says Jason. It wasn't until Christmas 2012, almost a year after the cat first started hanging around the pub, that Jason and his wife were startled by a noise in their bedroom. They looked in and "there he was, lying on our bed, snoring his head off".

Once in, he decided he rather liked it. He has since become a fixture downstairs in the bar, a homely place packed with wooden tables and leather armchairs, where he favours a stool next to "Bombardier" John, his favourite regular, who always feeds him treats. On Saturday nights during the football season he heads back upstairs to watch *Match of the Day* with Jason over a shared plate of pastrami. But it's not all leisure: "We've not had any problems with mice since he arrived," says Jason.

His only critic is the pub's chef Ayhan Sahin, who has made it his mission to cheer up Salem because he looks so sad. "But he's an old boy," says Jason. "He's allowed to be grumpy now and again." 🐾

Lenny & Patch

Best known for curry and salt-beef bagels, Brick Lane also has a fine little pub in the Pride of Spitalfields, home to an international ambassador among cats

AROUND 11.30AM EACH MORNING, Monday to Saturday, a small crowd of people gathers in a narrow, cobbled backstreet just off Brick Lane and mills around outside the modest frontage of the Pride of Spitalfields. As the guide of the East End Food Tour will announce, they are not there to meet its charismatic Liverpudlian landlady Ann Butler or sample the home cooking. Nor are they

there to learn about the diminutive pub's history: formerly the Romford Arms (it changed name in the 1980s), it was notoriously a haunt of Jack the Ripper suspect George Hutchinson.

They are not here for the décor (two small, parlour-like rooms, carpeted, slightly shabby) or even for the beer, although some of those present will probably sample at least one of the pub's

PRIDE OF SPITALFIELDS
3 Heneage Street, E1 (Aldgate East tube)
📞 020 7247 8933
🔲 LennyThePubCat
📘 The-Pride-of-Spitalfields

FACILITIES Piano, real fire, Sky Sports, vinyl night (Mon)

DRINKS Five real ales on draught

FOOD Pub classics including hot salt-beef sandwiches

well-kept ales, a point of pride since Ann and her late husband took over the pub some 25 years ago. No, what they are here for is Lenny the cat.

The large, 13-year-old tabby, who bears a distinctive pattern of dark brown, black and ochre on his back and face like a superhero cape and mask, knows it, too. At the same time every day, he makes his way down from upstairs to meet that morning's group and willingly accept his quota of rubs, pats, tickles and posing for pictures. "It's a role he's quite happily embraced in recent years," chuckles Ann.

Ann reckons his showy-off nature is down to his Liverpudlian charm: Lenny and brother Louis were picked up as one-year-olds from a shelter up in the north-west where Ann was visiting family.

"So sociable is Lenny that he has his own Twitter account. @LennyThePubCat"

Sadly Louis ran off early on and, while still spotted in the area for years after, become "too feral" for domestic pub life. Instead, Lenny now shares the pub with adopted brother Patch.

Patch – named for his mixed black-and-white colouring – prefers a quieter life to his housemate. He shuns the bar and tends to remain upstairs craving only the attention of Ann. Not so Lenny, who is completely at home in a packed room, which the Pride often is, patronised by an appealingly diverse mix of older East End locals and Shoreditch hipsters. Lenny is often curled in his favourite spot, on top of a red sofa near the fire. He will sometimes stir himself with the arrival of a favourite regular and take his place on a stool up at the bar. He also seems to enjoy the music

played by DJ Dean on Monday's vinyl nights when he will stretch out on the sofa in appreciation. In fact, so sociable is Lenny that he has his own Twitter account, @LennyThePubCat.

In Japan, however, both Lenny and Patch (who did eventually, albeit very briefly, show for his photograph, *right*) have equal status. They both feature in a book of British pub cats published in Tokyo, with the result that large numbers of Japanese tourists pop into the Pride in the hope of meeting its furry residents. They bring gifts and cards, and try to coax the cats into recreating the pictures in the book, especially the one on the front cover, which is of a certain tabby confidently addressing the camera from his bar stool. "Oh, that's so Lenny," says Ann. 🐾

Betty & Beyoncé

Very different in temperaments, two sisters rule the roost in sibling partnership at the Rose & Crown in Clapham

PUBLICAN DAVID WHITTAKER never expected to end up with cats. The way it happened was that he had this friend who was moving out of the country and she couldn't take her pets with her. So David agreed that if she really couldn't find anyone else he would take the cats. He didn't think it would come to that. "I thought it would be easy to get rid of two cute kittens," he says.

Of course, the friend failed to find any takers and David, landlord of Clapham Common's Rose & Crown pub since 2006, found himself reluctant carer to a pair of hyperactive one-year-olds.

There was something he felt he had to immediately address: their names. "They were called Beyoncé and Britney," says David. "I couldn't have cats that sounded like they'd been

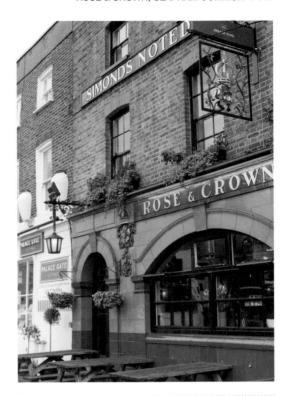

named by a five-year-old girl." Except that Beyoncé quickly proved that she really was the diva she'd been named after and so that name stayed. Britney became Betty.

Unsettled by the change of surroundings, the kittens initially spent their time hiding under the sofa in David's rooms upstairs. Little by little they sniffed around the new territory, decided it was safe and cautiously began venturing downstairs into the bar. After two weeks, they were bold enough to venture out among the benches and tables on the pub's forecourt, and promptly showed how much they appreciated David by doing a runner. "I thought I'd lost them," he says. Five hours later they came home, no word of explanation.

ROSE & CROWN
2 The Polygon, SW4 (Clapham Common tube)
📞 020 7720 8265

FACILITIES Three sports screens, outdoor seating

DRINKS Bar snacks only

FOOD Eight regularly changing ales, and a well-considered selection of whiskies and gins

That was five years ago. Happy to say, the cats are perfectly at home now, much-loved fixtures in the small pub on the north side of Clapham Common. In a neighbourhood dense with drinking options, the Rose & Crown tilts its hat at an older crowd, courtesy of an impressive line up of "grown-up" beers and friendly staff (including Estonian Tairi, *left*). Among the regulars, according to landlord David, is the guy whose real-life story inspired the musical *Billy Elliot*.

Like any sisters, the cats sometimes have their tiffs, but generally they are fiercely protective of each other, especially if another cat dares to trespass on their territory – if it's a dog doing the trespassing then they'll both usually scarper upstairs. Betty (black and white) is the more wary of the two and tends to avoid the bar area when it's busy; in contrast, Beyoncé (all black) is a bit of a tart and will cuddle up to anyone who pays her attention. "I always say that if there was a nuclear apocalypse tomorrow and they were left to fend for themselves, Betty would survive until the end," says David. "Beyoncé wouldn't last a day. She's too trusting and dumb."

If Beyoncé feels she's not getting enough attention, then she's not above putting in some

work to earn it. Her party piece, which she performs on the beer terrace out in front of the pub, is to jump from table to table until she's completed a full circuit. "She's like a show-dog," says barmaid Bonnie Bakkar. "It's pretty impressive."

The pair also make a pretty lethal mousing team. Having long since cleared the Rose & Crown of rodents they have moved on to help some of their neighbours with pest problems and currently they regularly act as night patrollers at the pub over the road, the Sun.

So have the girls converted David to a cat person yet? "No," he says. "But I have to admit, I have grown fond of them." ❧

Pork Pie & Scratchings

The cats may have strange names at Gospel Oak's Southampton Arms, but everything else about the pub is just spot on

FOR A WHILE, after they were adopted from the North London branch of Cats Protection in April 2010, the kittens were known as Pork Pie and Scratchings. Odd names, but their new home, the Southampton Arms – a stripped-down, retro-styled pub midway between Parliament Hill and Kentish Town – was well known for its meaty bar offerings, notably a well-stuffed roast-pork sandwich with apple sauce and crackling, and, well, nobody was able to come up with anything better.

The brothers – British shorthairs with piercing copper eyes and beautiful, silvery-blue fur, one cat slightly larger than the other, which is about the only way to tell them apart – were quick to settle in. Still, the pub's regulars (a disparate and

SOUTHAMPTON ARMS
139 Highgate Road, NW5 (Gospel Oak Overground or
Kentish Town tube)
📞 07958 780 073
🔲 SouthamptonNW5
🆆 www.thesouthamptonarms.co.uk

FACILITIES Beer garden, piano singalongs (Tue, Wed &
Sun), quiz (Mon), real fire

DRINKS Fantastic regularly changing line-up of
independent UK beers and ciders

FOOD Twist on old pub snacks: pork pies, sausage
rolls, roast pork sandwiches, scotch eggs

colourful bunch that takes in artists to labourers,
doctors and barristers) could never quite agree
on what to call them. Names that were tried out
on the kittens included Stripey and Non-Stripey,
Scamp and Scratch, Little and Big, Scaredy and
the Colonel, and Cheap and Costly. The latter
pairing came about a couple of years ago when
the larger of the two cats attempted an ambitious
jump onto a neighbour's wall and missed,
resulting in four broken ribs, a punctured lung
and a £1,000 vet's bill.

"I've lost count of the number of names they've
had now," says pub manager Ash Millard. During
the 2012 Olympics they even picked up some
Japanese nicknames. The pub, which was one of
the first in London to serve craft beers (all from

small, independent UK brewers, served in tankard glasses only), which plays its music on vinyl (or the piano) and which stubbornly remains strictly cash only, was written up as one of five "must-visit" places in a Japanese newspaper. The result was an influx of Japanese tourists, who not only merrily sampled the 18 different ales and ciders on tap (ask the bar staff for advice and try a couple of tasters), but also made a huge fuss of the pub's cats.

Not that the tourists would necessarily have been aware of it, but the Southampton has quite a colourful history. In the mid-19th century the building was part of the Southampton House Academy (an original sign still hangs on the now Grade II-listed building next door), a school that

The smaller cat likes to freak out dogs with what the pub manager describes as its "weird, fluffed-up, sideways zombie walk"

took in homeless boys from the streets. One hundred years later, according to local legend, it was one of the places that Bruce Reynolds, Ronnie Biggs and the rest of the gang used when plotting the Great Train Robbery of 1963. Later that decade, it was also one of the places where the Monty Python crew would meet up to brainstorm and scribble ideas for comedy sketches (Michael Palin still lives locally).

Today, it is the Southampton's cats that supply the comedic moments. The larger of the two often struts around on the back wall, occasionally with a rat in his mouth, caught beside the nearby railway lines. The smaller cat likes to freak out any visiting dogs by performing what Ash describes as its "weird, fluffed-up, sideways

THESE
BOTTLES
ARE
NOT
DRINKING
WATER

zombie walk", aimed straight at the terrified hounds. Otherwise, the pair love patrolling the piano, jointly exploring customers' shopping bags (by clambering inside them, naturally), bullying other neighbourhood cats or working on their attempts to open the door to the bar without any human aid (they are getting close).

Meanwhile, six years later, they continue to go without fixed names. Ash's two-year-old daughter Kitty Mae currently refers to them as Friendly and Unfriendly. "Except," says Ash, "she's always getting them mixed up, so I don't think those names will stick either." For the moment, then, Pork Pie and Scratchings (Scratch for short), it remains. 🐾

Nelson

The challenge at Kentish Town's backstreet Tapping the Admiral is to resist taking the pub's cat home with you

AS THE UK'S BIGGEST FREE SITE for classified ads, you can pretty much find most things on Gumtree. Which is why it was the first place Jay Hopkins – assistant manager of north London freehouse Tapping the Admiral – decided to look for a solution to his ongoing mice problem. Sure enough, he found his answer on the site, in the form of a two-year-old black-and-white-socked shorthaired cat that needed to be rehomed sharpish after someone's landlord decreed, "No pets". Fifty quid later and the pub had its mouser. But while it had a job – one it turned out to be extremely efficient at – the cat came without a name.

"Well, it had to be Nelson, didn't it?" says Jay. The name of the pub stems from the death of

TAPPING THE ADMIRAL
77 Castle Rd, NW1 (Kentish Town West Overground)
☎ 020 7267 6118
🐦 TappingAdmiral
📘 Tapping-the-Admiral
🌐 www.tappingtheadmiral.co.uk

FACILITIES Beer garden, quiz (Wed), live music (Thur), poker night, real fire

DRINKS It's a CAMRA award-winning freehouse with at least eight real ales on offer at all times

FOOD Classic British pub food with a £12 pie-and-pint special on Mon & Tue

Admiral Nelson at Trafalgar, whose body was returned home preserved in a barrel of brandy. Legend has it that during the voyage thirsty sailors snuck drinks from the cast, hence "tapping the admiral", meaning taking a sneaky drink.

No need to sneak around this Admiral though, which sits among some well-turned-out residential streets on the borders of Camden and Kentish Town, a short walk from Camden Lock. Hard to believe now, but until 2011 the building was a semi-derelict squat before it was bought by Kirk McGrath and Paul Davies, the gents behind popular community boozers the Pineapple, in nearby Leverton Street, and the Railway Tavern in Dalston. They fixed the place up and kitted it out with nautically themed bric-a-brac including thick

ropes hanging from the bar, framed paintings of pot-bellied, rosy-cheeked captains and vintage sea-faring-related signage. There is a poster for the 1973 film *The Last Detail*, with Jack Nicholson looking like he is auditioning for the Village People with bare chest, sailor's hat and large moustache.

It is very much a locals' pub, although it also pulls in beer aficionados from far and wide, as well as fans of folk and Irish music for the Thursday-night sessions. Pub and regulars alike are colourful going on eccentric, which might explain why the Admiral has served as the occasional meet-up venue for the members of Capital Beards, the London branch of the wonderfully hirsute British Beard Club.

Below Jack is Nelson's favourite spot, a counter top that catches the sun's rays whenever it puts in an appearance. "You wouldn't believe it now, but Nelson was really shy at first," says Jay. Not any more: he loves attention, which is just as well as he gets lots of it. If it is overcast or raining, he will swap his window seat for a miniature, mint-green chaise longue by the fireplace. At closing time he is moved, willing or not, to the covered patio area out back because if he stays inside he sets off the security alarms.

"He has the best life,' says Jay. "He eats, sleeps, struts around a bit and is constantly being stroked. People adore him. "I'm thinking about stealing Nelson if I leave," he adds. "Just for pest-control reasons, obviously." 🐾

Horacio & Woody

At Brixton's Trinity Arms two cats share space in a geek's den of Darth Vader fire pits and imperial stormtrooper graphics

IT TOOK TWO MONTHS and two visits to the vet to realise that Horacio was poorly named. That was when owners Rebecca and Ross Whittome were informed that their large, brown tabby was a she, not a he. "The name had stuck by that point so we kept it," says Rebecca. The other cat, Woodstock, or Woody for short, a small-boned tabby-Burmese cross, is definitely a he.

It was 2007, when the couple purchased the kittens after seeing an advert in a local shop window in Elton, Cambridgeshire. Actually, at first they purchased one kitten. "We got Woody first because he was just so sweet and friendly," says Rebecca. "But after a couple of weeks we thought it would be good for him to have some company." Enter Horacio and her quirks.

TRINITY ARMS
45 Trinity Gardens, SW9 (Brixton tube)
📞 020 7274 4544
🔲 TrinityArms
📘 Trinity-Arms-Brixton
🔳 www.youngs.co.uk/pubs/trinity-arms

FACILITIES Beer garden (front and back), quiz night (Thur), video-games room

DRINKS Young's beers

FOOD Traditional pub menu with daily specials

"She does this very strange, relentless screech and is very fidgety," says Rebecca. "And she's a passionate ankle biter." She is also an opportunistic thief: one time a customer left his lunch to go to the toilet and Horacio leapt onto the table, batted the top half of his burger to the floor, nabbed it and scarpered. Woody has his own strategy when it comes to parting customers from their meals: at the sound of cutlery being laid – a noise that will arouse him from even the deepest of sleeps – he will pad over to the table where the knives and forks are being placed and sit there patiently, waiting for the food that inevitably follows.

The Trinity is the cats' third pub. After Elton came a spell in Streatham, where the Whittomes

almost lost Woody. One day he disappeared and as the weeks passed his distraught owners gave up hope of ever seeing him again until a customer walked in and said, "Did you know your cat is on the roof?" And there he was – skinny and shaken, but alive and extremely pleased to see his rescuers who retrieved him with the aid of a ladder.

Had he been up there the whole time? Nobody knows. So the Whittomes were only slightly less worried when soon after moving to their new pub in Brixton, Woody disappeared again. This time he was gone for three weeks before he found his way back. That was seven years ago and he has never wandered off since. But why would he want to when he has a lovely

home like the Trinity, built in 1850 and named for a nearby almshouse, which gave refuge for poor women who professed to believe in the Holy Trinity. The pub was purchased by current owners Young's in 1911. It sits on a green square just off the high street, a little bit of rus in urbe in gritty Brixton. Inside it is high-ceilinged and wood-panelled, cosy in Farrow & Ball colours, but not too grown-up – check out the chalkboard messages reflecting the owners' idiosyncrasies, like the one that reads, "All dogs welcome – children must be on a leash."

And just wait until you see the backyard beer garden, which Ross, a graphic designer with a "big imagination", decorated to celebrate the release of *Star Wars: The Force Awakens*. Along with stormtrooper graphics and Darth Vader fire pits there is a bookable games room for online role-playing (Trinity Arms staff shirts bear the legend "Warlord of Draenor", which will mystify all but World of Warcraft fans). "Yeah, we're both a bit geeky like that," says Rebecca. "We just need to transform the cats into a couple of Wookiees and we're set." 🐾

Craig

**Mirror, mirror on the wall, who's the cutest
cat of them all? The answer possibly lies snoozing
at the Westow House in Crystal Palace**

IF THERE IS ONE THING on which the staff at
the Westow House pub are clear it's that they all
turn up at work each day for one reason: to cater
to the whims of Craig the cat. He is a ginger
stray who turned up one day about six years ago
and has made the pub his home ever since. If
the staff manages to keep the customers happy
as well, then that is a bonus.

It is a grand pub on one corner of the lively
Crystal Palace triangle, which commands
attention as you climb Westow Hill on the
five-minute walk up from the local station.

Inside, its big and high-ceilinged main room
is busy with a modish mismatch of retro furniture
– plump, red Chesterfield sofas, boudoir
lampshades – with, off to one side, a "recreation"

area with book-laden shelves, a pinball machine and foosball table.

Footie players need to keep an eye out for Craig because this is his domain. Beside the table and just inside the front door, is Craig's cupboard, a decent-sized hold-all for his treats (primarily Dreamies), along with his food bowl. Aged around eight or nine, he is a dead ringer for *Shrek*'s Puss in Boots and every bit as charming. But sometimes being adorable comes with its own problems. "Once, I was working in the restaurant and he kept getting under my feet," says bar worker and waitress Aga Prochniak. "Then I understood he wanted me to come to his food bowl where he wanted me to keep away his admirers while he finished his dinner."

WESTOW HOUSE
79 Westow Hill, SE19 (Crystal Palace Overground)
☎ 020 8670 0654
✆ westow_house
☐ Westow-House
Ⓦ www.westowhouse.com

FACILITIES Beer garden, board games, live music (Fri, Sun), pinball, quiz (Tue), reading library, table football

DRINKS Eight constantly changing real ales on draught mainly from microbreweries, plus extensive array of local and overseas craft beers

FOOD Full menu with a large dedicated dining room

As well as his personal space, Craig also likes meals to be punctual. Wherever he is in the neighbourhood – typically Crystal Palace Park across the road (venue for the first-ever cat show in the UK, back in 1871, don't you know) – he will always be back, sat outside the door at midnight Sunday to Thursday, and 2am on Friday and Saturday, seeing the last punters out and hungry for his nightly feed.

It's why he got so upset recently when there was a special function at Westow House for which the opening hours were extended to 3am. "He turned up as usual at 2am and was horrified to see so many people still in the pub," says Aga. "He wailed and wailed. It was clear that he wasn't at all happy about the late closing."

Apart from the occasional crankiness when hungry (and who isn't guilty of that?), Craig is a very loving cat who revels in all the attention he receives from the pub's punters (who can follow him on Twitter @pubcatcraig). He is a particular hit with women and has all the female staff completely wrapped around his paw. He is also a cat of mystery. Every night, according to supervisor Matt Fox, once Craig has been fed he is locked out of the pub by the last person to

leave. Yet every morning, he is there inside to greet whoever is opening up. "We've looked everywhere for some kind of cat-shaped hole," says Matt, "but we've yet to work out how he's getting in."

When not confounding people, Craig will be snoozing on one of the pub's chairs (it doesn't matter which one, he considers them to all be his). In good weather he's often out all day. "He's such a charmer, that it wouldn't surprise me if he was daylighting as another pub's cat, before coming here later for food," says Matt. "Let me know if you come across him in another pub." 🐾

Bud

The cat at Farringdon's White Bear may be named after a beer but he's tailless rather than legless

AT FIFTY QUID, Bud was a bargain. Especially for a tailless Manx cat with a fine grey-striped coat. Bought from a friend 12 years ago, he was the first cat the Marchant-Heatleys introduced to the White Bear, the pub they'd taken over a few years before. They named him after Budweiser beer.

He soon turned out to be not such a bargain when, at six weeks old, he fell off a chair and snapped his thigh in half. The vet presented his owners with three options: to amputate the leg; to pin it back together (at a pricey £500), or to put Bud down. "He was already without a tail, so we couldn't have him lose his leg as well," says Jonathon Marchant-Heatley, who manages the pub alongside dad, Oz. "And putting him down wasn't an option."

WHITE BEAR
57 St John Street, EC1 (Farringdon tube)
☎ 020 7490 3535
🅵 thewhitebearlondon
🆆 www.thewhitebearojs.co.uk

FACILITIES Dartboard, ginger Wednesdays, outdoor seating (limited), Sky Sports, upstairs function room

DRINKS Fine for lager drinkers but only two real ales on draught

FOOD Classic British pub food with special cheap lunch deals; summer BBQs

So the family coughed up. Two years later Bud was diagnosed with diabetes, requiring two costly injections a day to manage. He was also hit by a car after pelting out the door and straight onto busy St John Street, although fortunately he was only clipped, and the incident did at least have the benefit of scaring the life out of him and he has never attempted to cross the road since.

Still, according to Jonathon, Bud has more than earned his keep over the years, operating as auxiliary pub manager-cum-waste disposal unit. While he might come across as relaxed-going-on-comatose, Bud is always keeping an eye on things and every now and again will rouse himself from his favourite armchair and conduct a circuit of the pub – not that that takes very long, as the place is

barely bigger than the average living room. He is also always up for disposing of any waste fish skin from the kitchen.

Bud shares his home with three poodles – Bo, Poppet and new puppy Millie. Bud gets along just fine with the dogs, to the extent that the four of them even eat from the same bowl by the door. On the whole he is good with the customers, too, who are mostly local office workers (the pub generally stays shut at weekends when the offices are closed). Bud is happy to be petted, although only on the head and chin – he feels tummy and back rubs are overstepping the mark.

Every cat is entitled to pet preferences and Bud's is for iced water. He will jump up onto a stool, sit with his paws on the bar and stare intently at whoever is serving until he gets their attention. Their job is then to fill one of the drip trays with water, add a couple of ice cubes and place it in front of him. "He'll always wait a few minutes for the ice cubes to melt a bit," says Jonathan. "It's the only time he'll get up onto the bar, to go and sit by the ice bucket to remind the server that there's something missing."

He also has a soft spot for bags and if he sees a customer with one that looks particularly comfortable, he'll curl up on it. No one ever minds. It may be called the White Bear, but everyone knows it's Bud's gaff really. "We all work for him," says Jonathon. 🐾

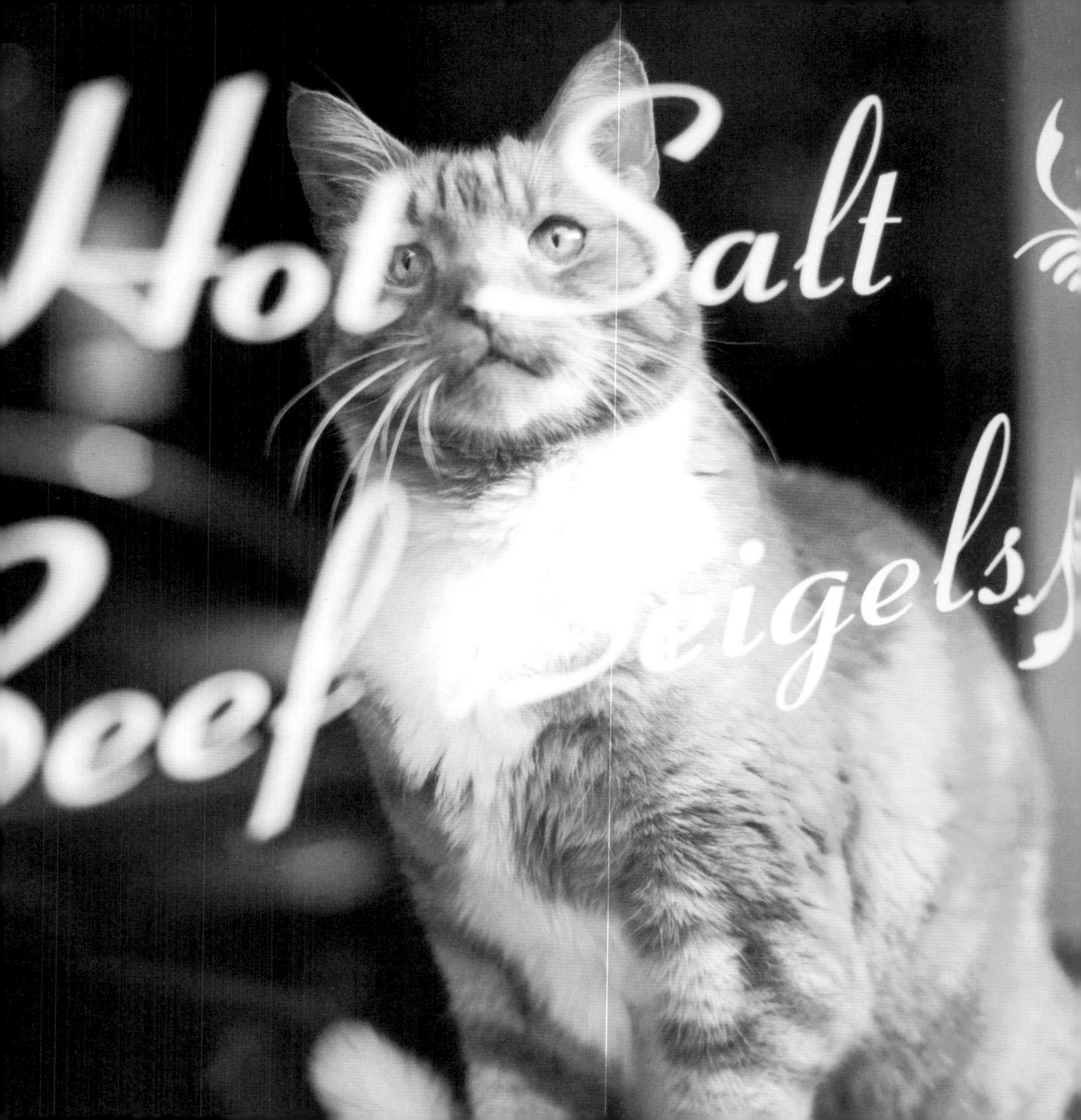
Hot Salt

Biscuit & Tea

Visitors are almost certain of Biscuit at Wapping's White Swan & Cuckoo but they rarely get Tea

THE WHITE SWAN & CUCKOO can not boast the pedigree of the nearby Prospect of Whitby or Town of Ramsgate, both pubs claiming to date from the 1500s. Nor can it match their claims to historical notoriety: the Prospect is where a young Charles Dickens allegedly used to drink; the Ramsgate is next to Wapping Old Stairs with its post to which pirates were tied to be drowned at high tide. However, in the age of the internet the White Swan & Cuckoo can claim more clicks than either of its more famous neighbours, all thanks to Biscuit.

That is Biscuit in the singular, not biscuits – as in Biscuit the cat. He is a ginger tom who likes to nap on the sill inside the front windows, a spot that catches the maximum sun and which also

WHITE SWAN & CUCKOO
97 Wapping Lane, E1 (Wapping Overground)
📞 020 7488 4959

FACILITIES Beer garden, big-screen sport, karaoke (Fri)

DRINKS Plenty of lagers, just one ale

FOOD Burger menu, pub classics, curry nights,
Sunday roasts

puts the absurdly oversized feline (he could be mistaken for a fox) on display to all passers-by.

"People walking along the lane outside will stop in their tracks when they see Biscuit," says Sal Djender, who runs the pub with partner Theresa. "Sometimes they'll come in, and often they'll take a photograph. There must be thousands of pictures of that cat circulating on the internet."

It was 13 years ago, and a year after the couple took over the White Swan & Cuckoo (Sal had formerly run a restaurant), that they decided it was time for a pet. A friend had a kitten for sale and that was Biscuit.

He took to pub life straight away and the pub's customers took to him, so 12 months later Sal

and Theresa took in two more kittens, shorthaired black-and-white brothers who they named Tea and Sugar. They did not take to their new home so well.

Sugar hated pub life so much that he eventually had to be rehomed. Tea tolerates his surroundings thanks to his coping strategy, which involves spending most of his time down in the basement hidden among the storage boxes. "It's almost impossible to find him if he doesn't want to be found," says Sal.

There are few places to hide in the large, L-shaped bar, which is a bit on the utilitarian side. It has a nice setting, though, round the corner from Wapping station on a lane lined with yellow-brick warehouses turned into flats.

So now the pub is neatly divided between upstairs cat Biscuit, who enjoys sitting up at the bar with the rest of the regulars and who particularly enjoys the Friday night karaoke sessions, at which he is always present, and basement cat Tea, who most people are not even aware exists. The two cats get on well. When it comes to meal times Biscuit will generally make sure his buddy eats first: "He'll sit next to Tea until he's finished eating before tucking in himself," says Sal.

Or maybe it's just his way of making sure Tea cleans the bowl. "Biscuit is so particular about cleanliness," groans Sal. "He won't touch his food if there's any sign of leftovers from the previous bowl in there." 🐾

 WHITE SWAN &

Hot Salt
Beef Beigels

THE
WHITE
SWAN
&
CUCKOO

More cats and pubs

NO WAY does this book include every pubcat in London. There are many more than we had room for. For example, we had to leave out Molly and Pip from the Blind Beggar on Whitechapel Road; Spider and Professor from the George Tavern on Commercial Road; and Sally from the Old Kings Head on Holywell Row (all in east London), to name just a few. Similarly, we never got to meet TC (as in Top Cat), the black-and-white cat who is a frequent visitor to the Cross Keys pub on Black Lion Lane in Stamford Brook, where he cadges chips from diners in the beer garden out back, or Alice, another black-and-white cat, who lives at the Sussex Arms just up from Twickenham Green. We also heard about but didn't make the acquaintance of the cat at the Kings Arms on Roupell Street in Waterloo, or the cats who are reported to frequent the Fox & Anchor in Smithfields and the Trafalgar Tavern in Greenwich.

Some of the pubs we did visit had cats that proved to be chronically camera shy. The Hoop & Grapes at 80 Farringdon Street, around the corner from Fleet Street and not far from St Paul's Cathedral, was one. It has a black-and-white cat named Guinness. She is a rescue cat who is skittish around people and stays clear of the bar. She does, however, like to sleep on a sofa in the second-floor public lounge. We found her there but the second she laid eyes on our photographer, Tim, she was off up the stairs to the safety of the landlord's top-floor flat and she would not come down again until we had gone.

Similarly, the cat at the Shakespeare's Head, behind Sadler's Wells Theatre at Angel. Ginger is a one-year-old who was adopted at the end of 2015 as a replacement for Whiskey, a much-loved tabby that had lived in the pub for around 20 years before she died a few years ago (the landlord claims her ghost now haunts the pub). The new kitten has yet to acclimatise to her new home and only ventures into the bar late at night after the last customers have drunk up and left. "It's early days," says landlord Jason Reynolds, "but we have faith that with time Ginger will perform just as well as Whiskey did in her role as the Shakespeare Head's new pub cat."

We had hoped to include Starsky and Hutch in this book, the two cats that live at the Boogaloo pub in Highgate. In the 12 years they have been resident at this raucous rock'n'roll venue, well known for its live music, the pair have won a reputation as hard-partying pusses, occasionally upstaging the acts and keeping punters company at the bar well into the early hours. Unfortunately, Starsky recently went AWOL and his partner has become reclusive in his absence.

There were other cats we had hoped to include that sadly took off to the great mousing-grounds in the sky before we got our project rolling. Foremost of these was the legendary Tom Paine, a great black puffball of a cat who lorded over the bar of the Seven Stars on Carey Street, behind Fleet Street's Royal Courts of Justice. He was notable for always wearing a chorister's ruff while on duty and used to take his off-duty naps stretched out in the window. Tom is commemorated in a poem written by a former regular that begins, *I'm Roxy's cat. I'm called Tom Paine / The Seven Stars is where I reign / No clever feline travels far / I live my life upon a bar*. Well, sadly no longer.

The Seven Stars has a new cat but he prefers to keep the company of his owner, landlady Roxy Beaujolais, in her rooms upstairs and avoids the bar. But who knows, caution may eventually give way to curiosity and he may take to the bar. In any case, we definitely recommend dropping in on one of London's most charismatic little pubs, cat or no cat – although, obviously, it would be so much better with a cat. 🐾

Thank you

A big thank you to Fanny Martin, who, with her partner, Pete, runs the splendidly named The Cat's Back (86-88 Point Pleasant, SW18). Historically, this was called the Foresters Arms until one day the pub cat, which had gone missing, returned and the pub got a new name. That was long ago and, despite the name, there's no cat there these days, but it is a very fine pub. Fanny allowed us to adopt the pub's whiskered-glass logo for our book.

Thank you also, of course, to all the pub owners and bar staff who gave up their time to help us with *London Pubcats*.

First published by Paradise Road 2016

Text © Paradise Road
Photographs © Tim White

A CIP catalogue for this book is available from the
British Library.

ISBN 978-0-9935702-1-6

Commissioned and edited by Andrew Humphreys
Designed by Gadi Farfour
Proofread by Omer Ali

Map on pages 10–11 by Julia Murray (jumurray.com)

Printed by C&C Offset Printing Co in China

PARADISE ROAD

www.paradiseroad.co.uk